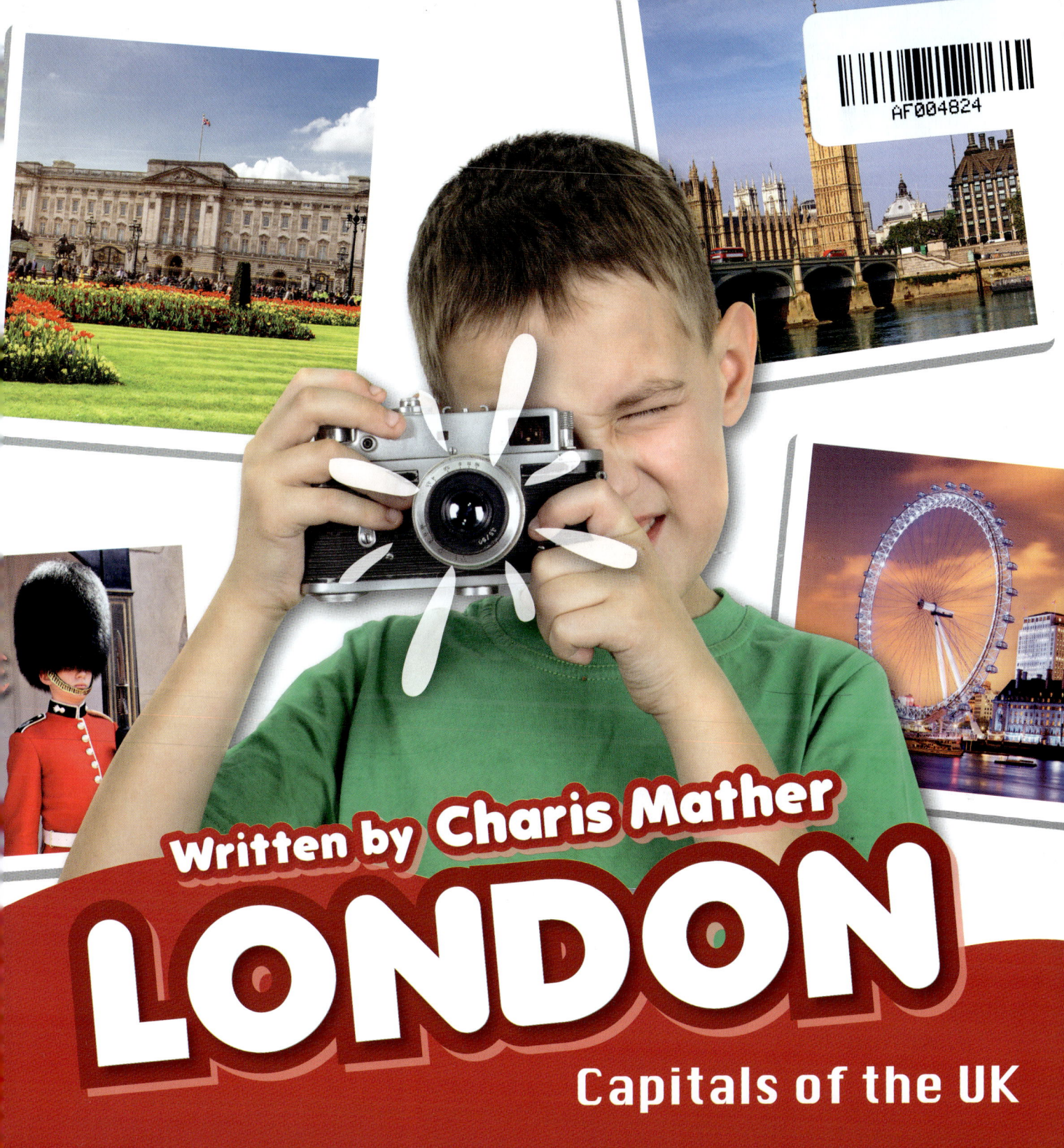

Written by Charis Mather

LONDON

Capitals of the UK

©2024
BookLife Publishing Ltd.
King's Lynn, Norfolk
PE30 4LS, UK

All rights reserved.
Printed in India.

A catalogue record for this book is available from the British Library.

ISBN: 978-1-80505-608-9

Written by:
Charis Mather

Edited by:
Noah Leatherland

Designed by:
Amelia Harris

All facts, statistics, web addresses and URLs in this book were verified as valid and accurate at time of writing. No responsibility for any changes to external websites or references can be accepted by either the author or publisher.

Image Credits

All images are courtesy of Shutterstock.com, unless otherwise specified. With thanks to Getty Images, Thinkstock Photo and iStockphoto. Cover – Happy Person, Madison Muskopf, PHOTOCREO Michal Bednarek, DaLiu, lunamarina. Recurring images – Voin_Sveta, ArtMari, Mutiah Sari Mustakim, Natasha Pankina, Liliana Danila. 2–3 – PHOTOCREO Michal Bednarek. 4–5 – 4kclips, Diego Sugoniaev. 6–7 – okili77, Kalinin Ilya, Ink Drop, Csaba Peterdi. 8–9 – Kiev.Victor, Marzolino, Rob Wilson. 10–11 – Pandora Pictures, Kiev.Victor, TasanP. 12–13 – wadstock, Alexander Chaikin, olavs, Philipp Dase, Sampajano_Anizza. 14–15 – Kurka Geza Corey, Jed Leicester, Chrispictures, Jeff Whyte, chrisdorney. 16–17 – Random Illustrator, I Wei Huang, Alexey Fedorenko, Gaid Kornsilapa. 18–19 – Anastacia - azzzya, Dmitry Tkachenko Photo, Thinglass, Roberto Marantan, Life In Pixels. 20–21 – ahmad agung wijayanto, 4zevar, Minaeva Emma, NoyanYalcin, Mark Anthony Ray, elRoce. 22–23 – Stuart Slavicky, Claudio Divizia, Click and Photo.

CONTENTS

Page 4	Welcome to London!
Page 6	My Capital, My Country
Page 8	London Long Ago
Page 10	Modern and Amazing
Page 12	Places from the Past
Page 14	Monuments to Remember
Page 16	Green Gardens
Page 18	Underground, Overground
Page 20	City of Culture
Page 22	Only in London
Page 24	Glossary and Index

Words that look like this can be found in the glossary on page 24.

Welcome to London!

London is a very <u>fast-paced</u>, busy city – and I love it! I also love taking pictures of this city to show my friends who have never been. This city is full of interesting places and people.

London is one of the most <u>multicultural</u> cities on the planet. The people in London have backgrounds from all over the world, not just from England.

People from London are called Londoners.

My Capital, My Country

England is the biggest country in the United Kingdom, and London is its capital city. The United Kingdom is made up of England, Scotland, Wales and Northern Ireland.

Scotland

Northern Ireland

England

Capital cities are where a country's important decisions are made.

London

Wales

Have you heard of the River Thames? It is a river that runs through London. It has had a big part in London's history. Many important places have been built along it.

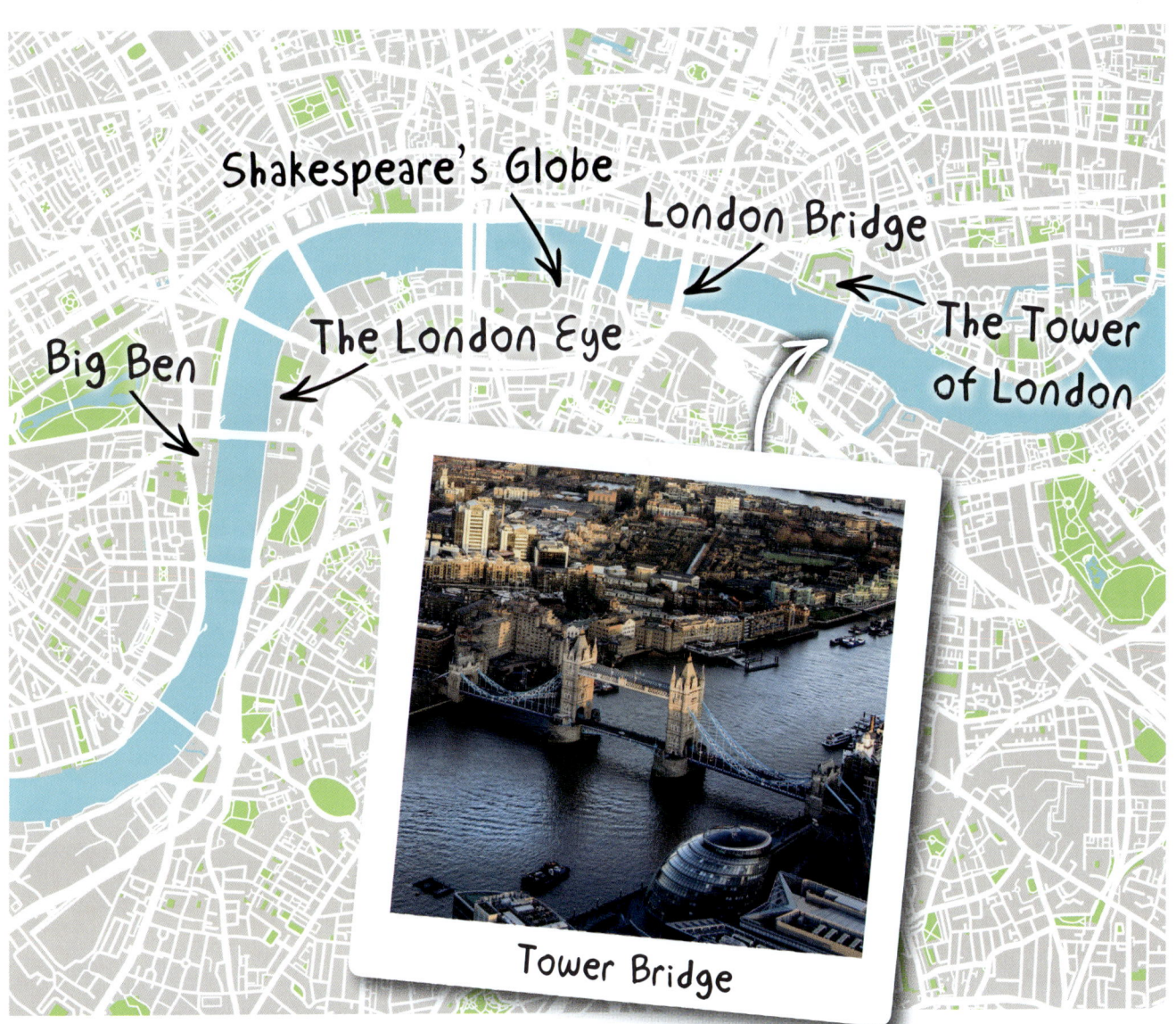

Tower Bridge

London Long Ago

London has changed a lot since the Romans <u>founded</u> it around 2,000 years ago. However, London is still full of old buildings that you can visit to see some of that history.

An old Roman wall in <u>modern</u> London

London in the past

It would be impossible for me to show you all of London's interesting places in one go, but I would love to teach you about some of them. Come and see my favourite spots!

London today

Modern and Amazing

London has a mix of old, historical buildings and new, modern structures. The Shard is a modern 72-<u>storey</u> building. It is the tallest building in the United Kingdom.

'Shard' is a word for a sharp piece of glass.

The London Eye is also called the Millennium Wheel.

The London Eye is a large wheel that people can ride to get a view of the city and some of its famous sights. It was built in 1999 to celebrate the new millennium.

Places from the Past

London has many old buildings that are still used today. They have hundreds of years of history.

The Tower of London

Westminster Abbey

The Houses of Parliament and the Elizabeth Tower, known as Big Ben

Buckingham Palace is home to the King of the United Kingdom. People come here to celebrate important royal events. The palace is protected by the King's Guard. The guards wear red jackets and tall hats.

Buckingham Palace was built in 1705.

Monuments to Remember

Monument to the Great Fire of London in 1666

Monuments are structures that are built to remember people or important events in the past, such as wars or big historical moments. There are monuments all over London.

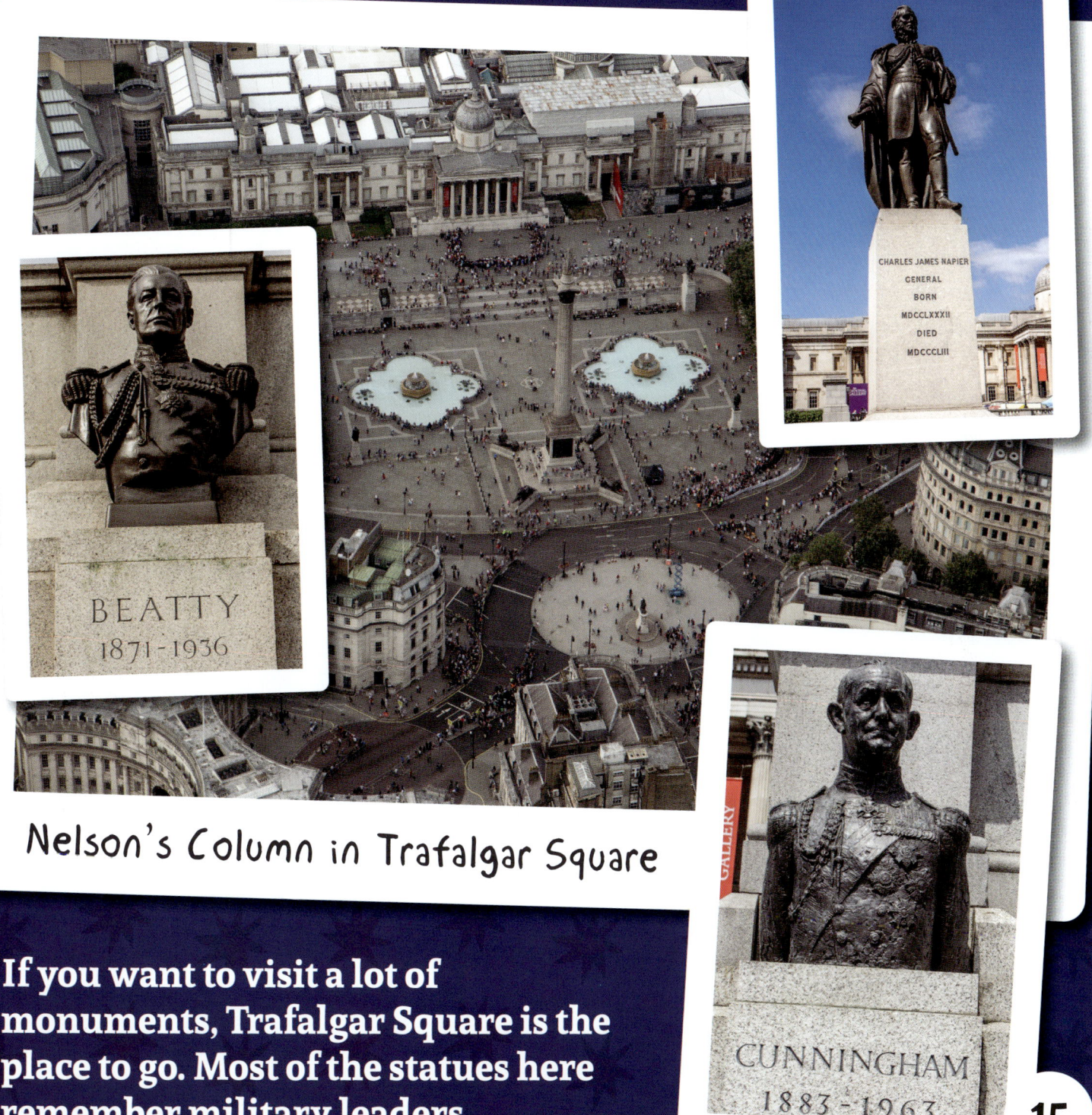

Nelson's Column in Trafalgar Square

If you want to visit a lot of monuments, Trafalgar Square is the place to go. Most of the statues here remember <u>military</u> leaders.

Green Gardens

Not all of London is buildings and statues. There are also plenty of green areas where you can enjoy nature. Hyde Park has lots of grassy areas, fountains and a lake.

Hyde Park

Kew Gardens

In Kew Gardens, you can see over 50,000 plants. Some of these plants are very <u>rare</u>. Many of them could not survive outside of the warmth of the large glass greenhouse that covers them.

Underground, Overground

There are many ways to get around London. The London Underground is the world's oldest underground railway system. It is used by millions of people every day and connects places all across the city.

The Underground is also called the Tube.

If you want to travel overground, you could take one of London's famous red double-decker buses. There are also lots of black taxis, especially in places that get lots of visitors.

City of Culture

London is famous for its art <u>galleries</u>, theatres and museums.

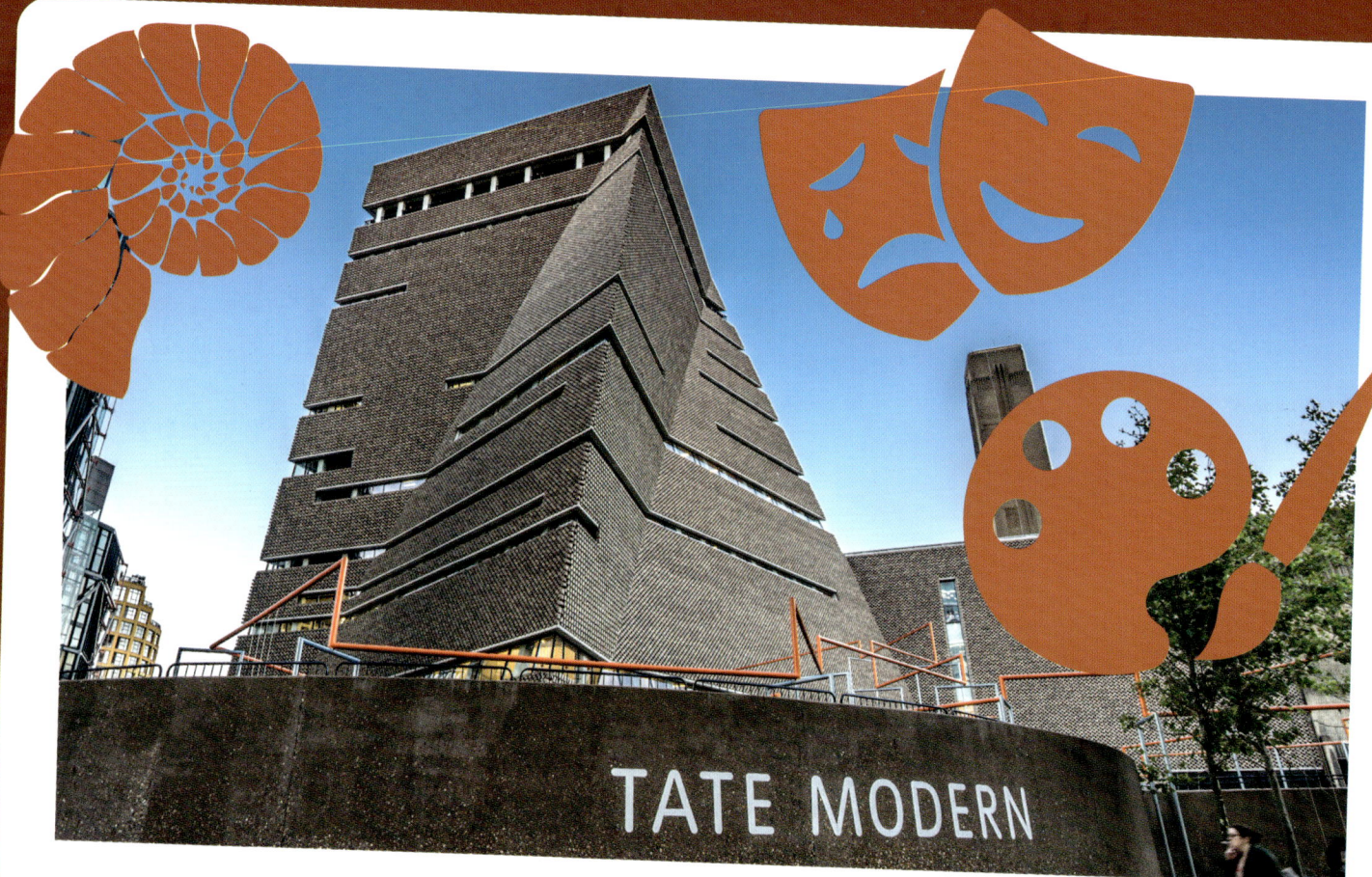

The Tate Modern is an art gallery. It has artwork from some of the world's most famous painters since 1900.

The West End is an area that is full of theatres. You can see performances here all year round.

The London Palladium

The Natural History Museum

London's many museums contain all kinds of important historical objects. Some are thousands of years old.

Only in London

There is no other city in the United Kingdom, or in the world, that is quite like London. There is so much to see and do here that I have not even told you about.

Carnaby Street

Shakespeare's Globe

Wimbledon

I have shown you a few of my favourite parts of this city through photographs, but it is definitely worth visiting London yourself. I hope that you enjoy being here as much as I do!

Take your own photographs to remember where you have been!

Glossary

fast-paced	moving quickly
founded	set up or started
galleries	places used for showing artwork
military	to do with the army
millennium	a thousand-year period
modern	to do with recent or present times
multicultural	to do with people from lots of different cultures or ethnic backgrounds
nature	to do with things in the world that are not made by humans
rare	hard to find because there are so few
royal	to do with a king, queen or their family
storey	a floor or level of a building

Index

art 20
bridges 7
glass 10, 17
history 7–8, 10, 12, 14, 21
monuments 14–15
museums 20–21
railway 18
rivers 7
theatres 20–21
towers 7, 12